Master catechist Bill Huebsch uncovers the heart of catechesis in twelve simple and powerful lessons. His clear writing invites the reader to ponder deeply the example of the Master. His gentle encouragement and practical learning process inspire confidence in even the most timid among us. If you are a catechist of any stripe, this book will change your ministry.

  NICK WAGNER, *director and cofounder of TeamRCIA.com*

As we reflect on our ministry as catechists, what could be better sources than the gospel witness of Jesus, the challenge of the GDC, and the vision of *The Joy of the Gospel?* Well, how about having all three woven together splendidly with the profound and practical insights of Bill Huebsch as he encourages us to know and follow Jesus, the master catechist? This book will support, nurture, and energize us, grounding us in the call and promise of our graced ministry.

  JANET SCHAEFFLER, OP
    Author, Adult Faith Formation and Retreat Facilitator

A magnificent book, abounding with profound spiritual wisdom presented in twelve creative lessons from Jesus, our master catechist. This wonderful resource offers exceptional guidance for those entrusted with responsibility for catechetical ministry. This is a book we all must read, reflect upon, and integrate.

  EDITH PRENDERGAST, RSC
    Director, Religious Education, Archdiocese of Los Angeles

---

In his easy, companionable style, Bill Huebsch offers catechists a short master course on the heart of catechesis. He embodies what he teaches. Like Jesus, he offers himself as a companion on our journey, passionate about the message he has received and eager to share it with us. This book refocuses us on our most important task—to proclaim and witness to the joy of the gospel by walking with our learners on a mutual journey of faith.

  JO ROTUNNO
    Former Publisher for RCL-Benziger

In this book, Bill Huebsch invites veteran and novice catechists alike to courageously approach their craft. With the accessibility we have come to expect from him, he invites us to get up close and personal with Jesus, the master catechist, and to open ourselves to the transforming grace of God unfolding in our ministry. Huebsch reminds us that as we open our hearts to the possibilities God offers, we tap into the wellsprings of joy that are so characteristic of the true catechist.

   ❧ **Fr David Loftus**
      Pastor for Our Lady of Lourdes Church in Northridge, CA

Bill Huebsch again demonstrates his unique ability to get quickly and simply to the heart of the most complex matters. In this clear volume, he quickly gathers his readers at the feet of Jesus, the master catechist, and lets the gospel and the church remind catechists old and new that their only job is to lead learners to Christ. This inspiring book is a must for everyone called to be a catechist.

   ❧ **Cullen Schippe**
      President and publisher, Pflaum Publishing Group

The ESSENTIAL CATECHIST'S BOOKSHELF

Jesus
THE MASTER CATECHIST

TWELVE LESSONS
from JESUS *on*
BEING *a* CATECHIST

Bill Huebsch

ACKNOWLEDGMENTS

The GDC in Plain English. St Paul, MN: PastoralPlanning.com, 2013. Available in PDF only.

Unless otherwise noted, all Scripture is from the New Revised Standard Version Bible, copyright 1989, Division of Christian Education of the National Council of the Churches of Christ in the United States of America.

The material from Pope Francis and *The Joy of the Gospel* is summarized here unless it appears in quotation marks.

TWENTY-THIRD PUBLICATIONS
1 Montauk Avenue, Suite 200, New London, CT 06320
(860) 437-3012 » (800) 321-0411 » www.23rdpublications.com

ISBN: 978-1-62785-062-9
Library of Congress Catalog Card Number: 2014955409

Contents

INTRODUCTION

"Every catechist needs to learn from a good catechist," one of my theology professors once told us. We learn how to provide faith formation or catechesis by watching others. We see them guiding their students, forming and shaping their message, and allowing their own faith to be evident—and we absorb what we see and hear. We listen as they address their students with love and care. We learn how to turn our own skills for teaching into the art of catechesis.

Those experienced catechists who are given the task of guiding and showing others the way are usually called "master catechists." They've often given many years to this ministry and have become models for us all.

Well, there is no better master catechist than Jesus himself. In this book, we will examine how we can become better catechists ourselves by following his example. We'll learn to allow people to gather around us, we'll learn to speak clearly of the Father's love, and we'll learn to extend the endless forgiveness of God to our students. We'll learn to pray for our students, to lead them to the brink of the paschal mystery, and to trust in divine grace for the rest.

What we will treat in this book is based on three major sources. First, we will turn at length to the gospel accounts of Jesus, the master catechist and teacher. In the gospels, we learn very specific lessons on what it means to pass on the faith from one person to another—lessons from Jesus on being a catechist. Second, we will learn from articles 160-173 of *The Joy of the Gospel* by Pope Francis. This section of the pope's document is directed to us as catechists and teachers. Finally, we will draw heavily from *The General Directory for Catechesis in Plain English* (the GDC, for short). From the GDC we learn the skills and methods for making these lessons come alive for us in the actual place where we teach.

The first lesson we will consider is the one from which the title of this book is drawn, namely, that we should imitate Jesus in our ministry of catechesis. He is the master catechist and model for us all. In order to imitate Jesus, we must examine his style and methods as we find them in the gospels.

The second lesson for us as catechists is that one way to imitate Jesus is to cultivate the soil of our students' lives and hearts to make it fertile and receptive for the seeds of faith. We plant these seeds and water them, but the Holy Spirit stirs up faith in the hearts of our learners so that the seeds grow and yield a great harvest.

Our third lesson is that it takes courage for our students to trust Jesus and surrender to his love. They and we must let go of all other securities, including money, power, fame, or popularity. It's not easy, but we know that Jesus does not disappoint. He is waiting with open arms.

After this lesson, we will take our first "prayerful pause" (other such pauses will follow) to learn how to prepare our hearts to teach by allowing Jesus to wrap his open arms around us. Whenever we are learning from Jesus, it is good to pause in order to allow our encounter with him to sink deeply into our consciousness. Like our students, we too need to make the gospel more than "head knowledge." We need to integrate the Good News into the whole of our being—and these prayerful pauses will help us do that.

The fourth lesson from Jesus is that faith leads to spiritual knowledge. We grow to know and trust that God is with us. The light will beat out the darkness, love is stronger than hate, and joy comes from dying to ourselves. These are things we *know*. We have the assurance of faith.

Our fifth lesson is that we believe Jesus will love and heal us no matter what. And the key in that sentence is the final phrase: *no matter what.* Nothing can separate us from the love of God in Jesus, as Romans 8:35 points out, but believing that can be very difficult. Our students' lives are filled with occasions on which they have missed the mark and not been fully loving. And yet Jesus forgives through the ministry of the church.

Lesson six is that our task is to walk with each learner and help each one go and meet Jesus, to encounter him today. Pope Francis asks us to become companions to our students, and lesson six teaches us how to do that in the style of Jesus.

After the sixth lesson we will pause again, this time to learn how to let the Holy Spirit help us prepare to teach.

The seventh lesson is that we are called to become servant-catechists. We are called to wash the feet of our students by serving their needs. This requires patience, kindness, and an attentive posture toward each student—all of which is not an easy task for us.

Lesson eight teaches us that our chief task is to lead our students to Jesus' loving heart. This is how they will "see Jesus." This lesson teaches us that the Christian journey is more about growing in love than about understanding theology.

In lesson nine, Jesus the master catechist reveals to us that God implants within us the gift of grace, and only by that grace can we respond in faith. We help our students cooperate with that grace; their faith will save them.

And here, after the ninth lesson, we will pause again, taking the time to learn how to pray for our students one by one, listening to what God may be asking of us in regard to them.

Our tenth lesson comes from Jesus through Pope Francis: "On the lips of the catechist," the pope tells us, "the first proclamation must ring out over and over: 'Jesus Christ loves you; he gave his life to save you; and now he is living at your side every day to enlighten, strengthen, and free you.'" This lesson helps us keep this good news in the forefront of all we teach.

The eleventh lesson teaches us that the purpose of continually reminding our students that Jesus loves them, that he died for them, that he forgives them, and that he now walks with them, is to tease out a response of faith; faith is our goal. And not merely enough faith to get through First Communion or confirmation but enough for a lifetime of faith-filled living as Catholic Christians.

Lesson twelve is that when we really listen carefully to our students with our whole heart, we open the doorway of faith for them. Only in letting them process and absorb what we teach can we lead them to Jesus. And Jesus himself had this openness of heart; once again, he is our master catechist.

And finally, in conclusion, we will pause together for the last time, learning how to pray both before and after we teach. We want to find a calm moment in our otherwise very busy lives in order to let God's grace flow through us in our ministry.

GROUP USE

If you are using this book in a small group setting and want to process each lesson a bit more, consult the Study Guide for Group Use at the end of the book to learn about a method for doing that.

A FINAL THOUGHT

It was early in Jesus' career as a catechist that he began to realize his need to take time away from his students and disciples, time alone to pray. At the end of chapter 4 in the Gospel of Luke, we find him doing just that. Time and again in the gospels, this desire to sneak in a little time for quiet, solitude, and prayer characterized Jesus' work. But his prayer always led him back to his work as a catechist.

We too need time for prayer away from the busyness of daily life. As prayer did for Jesus, our prayer will also lead us into our ministry of leading others to faith. Such times of prayer and reflection help us become authentic; we must live the faith that we share with others.

The crowds of eager learners that pressed in on Jesus and his disciples found him to be absolutely authentic too. He did not teach one thing and then do another. He "practiced what he preached," as the saying goes. And his message was not an easy one: love your enemies, give away your money, turn the other cheek, forgive seventy times seven times.

What kept his message fresh and compelling for the crowds (and for us) provides us with the key to understanding these twelve lessons. The gospels are both absolutely attractive to us and to our students and yet they are also terribly challenging. We want to live by the teachings of Jesus. We know it is right. We know it leads to happiness. And we know it leads to an eternity of love and light in the reign of God. And yet…it is also frightening. We know we must die to ourselves, but we don't like dying. We know we must be good to those who hate us, yet we fear we will be considered fools. So what Jesus teaches us as catechists is both compelling and frightening. It is a mystery. We are drawn to it while we are also repelled by its demands.

In chapter 5 of Luke, the crowds have mobbed Jesus to the point where, in order to be heard, he gets into Peter's fishing boat, rows out from shore a little way, and teaches people while seated in the stern. I'm sure his disciples watched all this with both the fascination we just described and also the horror of seeing such crowds making demands on them—the mystery of faith both attracting them and repelling them at the same time. Jesus seemed to read the hearts of Peter and his friends because, when he had finished teaching that day, he asked them to row out into deeper waters where they had just spent the entire night fishing without much to show for it. There, at Jesus' request, they put down their nets into the waters and caught such a huge number of fish that they had to call for help to wrangle them to shore. The text tells us that they were amazed! And Peter, knowing he was not worthy because of his sinfulness, begged Jesus to just leave him alone. But Jesus would have none of that nonsense and instead built his church on these guys, whom he directed to start fishing for people.

These twelve lessons from Jesus our master catechist will have the same impact on us if we let them sink deeply into our hearts and our classrooms. We will find the power of God in them. We will find ourselves calling for help when our catch is too large for us to handle. We will be greatly attracted to the teachings and methods of Jesus, drawn to them as the disciples and the crowds were, but we may also fear that we are not really able or worthy to do this amazing ministry. Fear not, my friends! Jesus is calling us to be fishers of our students. Let's go!

Jesus is the master catechist

Throughout his ministry among us, Jesus accompanied his disciples, apostles, and all of his followers on their journeys of faith. He gently and lovingly led them to meet his Father and come to know how much God loves them and how often God forgives them. As we meet Jesus going about his daily work, we learn a great deal about what it means to be catechists and teachers today.

The General Directory for Catechesis (the GDC, for short) refers to Jesus' teaching style as "the teaching style of God." Here is what the GDC says in article 137:

> *Jesus Christ is the first catechist.*
> *He was not only teacher but also friend*
>   *to his disciples.*
> *He lived what he preached.*
> *He asked opportune questions*
>   *and explained privately to his disciples*
>   *what he taught the crowds.*
> *He introduced them to prayer.*

> *He sent them as missionaries*
> *and sent his Spirit with them.*
> *Indeed, this is the "teaching style of God,"*
> *the model for all we do.*

There is much we can learn from Jesus as the master catechist. The GDC goes on to say in article 140 that Jesus is the perfection of this divine teaching style. In Christ, the disciples learned how to pass on the faith: calling the poor and rejected to them, proclaiming the reign of God, living a delicate but strong love that liberated them from evil and promoted a common life, taking on a lifestyle that reflects this teaching—the teaching of hope in the kingdom and of charity to one's neighbor.

The GDC

The General Directory for Catechesis is a papal document published in 1997. It had been called for at the Second Vatican Council in the "Decree on the Bishops' Pastoral Office in the Church," article 44. It is the guide for all we do in catechesis and faith formation.

To help a person grow in faith, which is our task as catechists, means that we must help our students summon the courage to reach out to Jesus. We invite them to come to Jesus, just as he welcomed people to come to him during his public ministry. The relationship of our students to Jesus creates the basis for prayer and the foundation on which they can learn to live as Jesus teaches us to. The ministry of the church can then become the context for living that faith in daily life.

We know that God touches the hearts of our learners through the Holy Spirit to lead them into ever-deeper intimacy with Jesus. In this spiritual process, God transforms the events in the lives of our students—both the happy times as well as the more difficult times of life—into lessons of liberation and wisdom. This is what we catechists are called to help our students experience.

We help our students hear the divine call to become disciples of Jesus. As disciples, they learn prayer, they celebrate liturgy, they include the poor at every level of their lives, they invite and welcome others to follow Jesus, and they study and learn about their faith.

Disciple

A disciple is a person who embraces the teachings of Jesus and lives by them. The word comes from the Latin verb *discere* meaning "to learn." Catechists are disciples, and our students are called to become disciples too.

This all happens now in the context of the church. The church is a sacrament to the world, a sign of the presence of Christ. When outsiders and strangers see us as the church, they should see the forgiving, loving presence of God in their midst. We are a living catechesis. When we worship and celebrate together, when we tend to the poor and rejected, when we work for peace and justice, then we are building the reign of God. And we learn how to do this from Jesus himself.

The first lesson, then, is that we should imitate Jesus in our ministry of catechesis. He is indeed the master catechist who teaches us all. In order to imitate Jesus, we must examine his style and methods.

In the Gospel of Luke, Jesus does a lot of his teaching at meals. Meals are his favored way to offer both intimacy and the example of good hospitality. He laces such meals into a

9

very busy schedule. In chapter 18, for example, we find him teaching in parables day after day, blessing children, taking time to help a wealthy young man realize what an obstacle his wealth is to his own eternal happiness, and giving sight to yet another blind fellow. Jesus is getting close to entering Jerusalem for the last time, where he knows he will face his enemies; he continues to try to explain this to his disciples, but they just do not get it. "They understood nothing about all these things," the text tells us in 18.34.

So in the midst of all this, with trouble brewing just ahead, Jesus enters the small town of Jericho, seventeen miles outside of Jerusalem. We are about to witness one of the most personal and teachable moments in Jesus' entire ministry. At first glance, this incident may seem like nothing special, like something we might encounter with any of our own students, but it is a strong lesson for us. Jesus is walking along the road and, as usual, there are crowds of people trying to get near him. In the midst of this, he spots a short guy named Zacchaeus sitting up in a sycamore tree. Partly as a way of teaching a catechetical lesson, and partly because he loves a good meal, Jesus calls Zacchaeus out of his perch and invites himself to supper. "Who has time for this?" his disciples must have thought. "We're busy!"

But off Jesus goes, leaving the religious leaders behind complaining about how he dared to have supper with a known sinner.

APPLYING THE LESSON

You don't have to be sinless and perfect for Jesus to love you or call you to live selflessly. In fact, the more aware you are of your own sins, the more ready your heart will be to walk with Jesus. As we approach our students with this incredibly good news, we learn from Jesus not to be shy about calling our students out of their own sycamore trees and inviting them to give half their possessions to the poor.

In this lesson, we learn that Jesus is both the message itself as well as the conveyor of the message. As catechists, we now become his hands and feet, his mouth and ears. We introduce our students to the amazing love of God, and we do it as Jesus did, by calling them forth from the midst of their sinfulness and showing them how much we love them. Even if this means going to their homes for supper, it's what we do.

We prepare our students as a farmer prepares the soil

One of the most outstanding features of Jesus as master catechist is that he always helped his disciples and other followers to receive his teaching. He did this in the same way a farmer would prepare soil for planting the seed that would grow into a crop of wheat. The soil must be ready to receive the seed: rocks moved out of the way, weeds kept under control, and the soil made warm and wet so the seed can germinate. The Gospel of Mark can teach us more about this.

It had been a busy few days for Jesus and his entourage, according to the opening chapters of Mark. Jesus had been "in his public life" only a little while, but he had wasted no time. He worked with a strong sense of urgency. He healed a leper, helped a paraplegic get up and walk, had dinner with some low-life tax collectors, and challenged the rules about the Sabbath. The crowds had likewise quickly discovered the power in Jesus' teachings and were coming out to see him in great numbers. Were they merely curious? Or were they ready to follow and become disciples? Jesus was their catechist, and he seemed to know that doubt was in their hearts. Faith, he taught them in Mark 4, is like seed that a farmer plants. Some of the seed takes root, like the word of God in people's hearts, while other seed sprouts and dies, or doesn't sprout at all. "Are you listening to this," he asked them, "really listening?"

Catechist

A catechist is a person who lives his or her faith convincingly and teaches others to grow in their faith. The word *catechist* comes from a Greek verb meaning "to teach by word of mouth."

Your life should be like the good earth into which my teachings fall, he told them. Let what I teach grow in you like sturdy plants, and not only for your sake but also so that it will produce a yield of kindness, good works, and a light for the world. Jesus knew that the people of his time were filled with concerns for daily life, security, shelter, and other demands. Faith was not everyone's first priority.

As catechists and teachers, we know that our students are like this. Their hearts are torn by many distractions and diversions. The winds of the culture in which they live blow first toward one set of values and then toward another. The messages they receive are too numerous to fully list, but some have to do with possessions and consumerism. They're encouraged to get all they can, to buy whatever they want, and to seek happiness through consumption. "Surely the next hot item," they're told, "will fulfill you and make you happy."

Other messages have to do with popularity. Following the lead of the invisible leaders becomes a goal above all others. Whatever the trend is now, even if not in their own taste, they feel they must follow it or fall out of favor with the "in crowd," whoever that is at the moment. This pursuit of popularity can lead to strange and deadly choices if it involves being too thin, too high, or too tan.

Some messages have to do with being in power, others with knowing unlimited pleasure, living in the right place, or being seen with the right people. The great danger in today's world, Pope Francis reminds us in article two of *The Joy of the Gospel*, is that we will allow ourselves to be overcome by consumerism of this sort. If we do that, he warns, our hearts will be set on frivolous pleasures, and our consciences will be blunted. We must make room for others and especially for the poor. We must learn to listen for God's voice, for the quiet joy of being in God's presence and love.

The Joy of the Gospel

The Joy of the Gospel is an apostolic exhortation written personally by Pope Francis and published in 2013. It expresses his hope and dream for the modern church. It provides a blueprint for our ministry.

As catechists and teachers, we are offering our learners an avenue to happiness and fulfillment that entails letting go of all these false and empty promises. We are inviting them to do something unheard of in most cultures: to die to themselves and to learn the art of self-giving love. We have a great challenge, because our only promise to them is that the choice we offer will lead them to enormous and eternal happiness. We are offering our students a pathway to true and deep joy, but it will always take some time for them to understand this, trust in God, and follow.

Hence this lesson: we gradually prepare their hearts and

lives to receive the word of God and trust in it. This gradual becoming-able-to-see-and-understand is also what we ourselves experienced when faith was new to us.

Jesus, too, knew that his message was one that would require time to absorb, and he was willing to help the people whom he met. Just as a farmer plants the seed and then tends his crop, so Jesus tended the belief of his followers. He warned them not to be fooled by so-called wise advice that told them they could be happy aside from his teaching. Let faith grow, he seemed to be saying, as a tiny pine nut grows into a large tree. He and his disciples spent a great deal of time together, sorting this all out, going over everything time and again, and working out the mysteries one by one until they seemed ready.

But even then, even when they seemed to have gotten it, Jesus still had more to teach. The storms of life rage around you, he taught one day in a boat on rough waters in Mark 4:40. Only faith, only believing in love, only holding fast to one another, can get us through the tough times. The lessons from Jesus just kept coming.

WHAT IT MEANS FOR US

And this is also how it is in our ministry of catechesis. The lessons are endless, and the learning is lifelong. We never fully plumb the mystery of God. We are always learning how to live our faith more fully. This entails peering into our lives as we examine our consciences to find the selfishness and sinfulness that are there, confess that, and celebrate forgiveness through the ministry of the church. It entails peering into our pocketbooks to see how much money we have hidden and kept for our own selves and how much we have put to work to feed the poor, cure the sick, and build the reign of God. It entails peering into our relationships in order to forgive our enemies, love our dear ones more selflessly, and make sure we have created a way for the last to become the first.

The second lesson for us as catechists is that we imitate Jesus when we cultivate the soil of our students' lives and hearts to make it fertile and receptive for these seeds of faith. We plant these seeds and water them, but it is the Holy Spirit who stirs up faith in the hearts of our learners so that the seeds grow and yield a great harvest.

Jesus spent his life as this kind of catechist. You really can't open the gospels without stumbling onto a passage in which we hear Jesus teaching. In Mark 2, for example, the crowds had discovered Jesus and were eager to learn from him. They so crowded the house in which he was staying that some people dug through the roof to get close to him. They brought with them a paralyzed man. The lesson Jesus taught that day is that God forgives us, and God's forgiveness heals us. We need not fear that God will disappoint us, he taught the crowds.

Later he was out near the sea, which we know he loved. "The whole crowd gathered around him," the text tells us in verse 13, "and he taught them." And this is precisely the amazing and noble ministry of catechesis to which we are called. For us, it may be the young children in elementary school who gather around us. Or it may be youth from the parish as they prepare for a lifetime of faith. Or perhaps it is adults gathering in the RCIA or in an adult education program. Whomever it is, they gather around us as catechists, we stand in their midst, and, like Jesus, we prepare their hearts and teach them.

It takes courage to seek out Jesus and trust him

Jesus went about his ministry of healing, teaching, and gathering people to hear the word, and he did this together with his disciples. Meanwhile, some of the religious leaders of the day were busy arguing over the theology of Jesus' teachings. Jesus seemed to burst through their thin walls of rules and regulations, reaching out to the people with mercy, love, and compassion. He taught the people to practice self-giving love, to be generous, to forgive each other, and to trust in God. Such simple and open faith seemed to go against the doctrine of the day, and some religious insiders were not very happy about it.

One of the people listening to all this was a local leader of the synagogue named Jairus. Like many in the crowds around that area, he had been following the attention that Jesus was getting. There were stories of people being healed, of a new attitude toward faith, and even of demons being controlled by the faith of this man, Jesus. Jairus had not yet met him, even though he'd heard a lot about him.

In our ministry of catechesis and faith formation, many of our students are in this exact position. They have heard a lot *about* Jesus; they have listened as his teachings were explained, sometimes clumsily, by church leaders; and they have known or sensed that something unique and powerful emanated from him. But they have not yet actually *met or encountered* him.

Meeting someone in person is very different from merely knowing about him or her. Encountering someone is personal and life-changing for both people. There is risk involved in such encounters, especially if you allow another to enter into your heart. Simply watching Jesus from across the town square was safe; many people stopped at that level of knowing him.

In *The Joy of the Gospel,* Pope Francis seems to sense this. In the opening articles of the document, he begins by calling us to cross the town square and approach Jesus, just as Jairus wanted to do. "Don't just watch from afar," Pope Francis seems to say. "Get up close and personal."

"I invite all Christians, everywhere, at this very moment, to a renewed personal encounter with Jesus Christ…" he wrote in article 3. "I ask all of you to do this unfailingly each day. No one should think that this invitation is not meant for him or her…"

Jairus and his daughter

The story of Jairus and his daughter is told in three gospels: Matthew 9:18–26, Mark 5:21–43, and Luke 8:40–56. That this story appears so often tells us that it was a very well-known and important story for the early community.

Jairus seemed to hear in his own heart what Pope Francis is now inviting us all to do. Jairus had a serious and very personal problem. It had nothing to do with the debate going on in religious circles about Jesus' theology. It had to do only with his beloved daughter who lay dying in their home. So, risking everything, including his own reputation, Jairus went to meet Jesus. He asked Jesus to come with him to the bedside of his dear child. And Jesus agreed to go. As Pope Francis reminds us so forcefully in *The Joy of the Gospel,* article 3, Jesus does not disappoint. When we go to him, he responds with love; the only response he ever gives us is love.

Here is our third lesson: it takes courage to go to Jesus. We must let go of all other securities, including money, power, fame, or popularity. It's not easy, but we know that, as Pope Francis said above, Jesus does not disappoint. He is waiting with open arms, and this is the message we pass on to our students.

I'm sure Jairus was overjoyed that Jesus agreed to visit his house and his daughter. Such joy is also the promise we make to our students. If they trust in God and go to him, if they give themselves over to the journey of faith and walk with Jesus, they will experience true and deep joy. No one else in the marketplace of potential fulfillment can offer this joy.

Prayerful pause:
Prepare your heart to teach

You'll need about fifteen minutes to complete this exercise. Find a quiet place to sit; turn off your mobile phone. Begin by turning your heart toward Jesus. He stands beside you every day, and when you turn to him, he will welcome you with love.

1. Pause and think about your journey of faith from your birth up to the present moment. (You may want to jot down a few notes as you proceed here.) Where were you baptized? What was your childhood faith experience like? When and where did you receive your First Holy Communion? Who had great influence on your spiritual formation? Who were your teachers and companions? What turning points did you experience as you passed through the years of your youth and young adulthood? How did your adult faith grow and mature? What parishes have you belonged to? What ministries have you done in those parishes? What are your spiritual hungers like today? What challenges your faith today? What strengthens it?

2. (Complete this paragraph.) As I think back over my life, I see that I have not always given myself heart and soul to Jesus. Contrary to what Saint Paul suggested in Galatians 2:20, I have not always allowed Christ to live in me. I have not always trusted that Jesus would love me, because I know I have done things that create a distance between me and Jesus, including these:

3. (Complete this sentence.) I have been afraid to give Jesus my whole heart because I fear this:

4. (Create a short list.) But I do believe I am called to return to Jesus now. I hear this call embedded in my life, in these people, events, or situations:

5. Now let us pray, in the words given to us by Pope Francis in *The Joy of the Gospel*, 3:

> "*Lord, I have let myself be deceived; in a thousand ways I have shunned your love, yet here I am once more, to renew my covenant with you. I need you. Save me once again, Lord, take me once more into your redeeming embrace.' How good it feels to come back to him whenever we are lost! Let me say this once more: God never tires of forgiving us; we are the ones who tire of seeking his mercy.*"

6. You may wish to take this with you into the sacrament of reconciliation, a visit with your spouse or dear friend, private prayer, or a conversation with a spiritual director.

Faith provides us with spiritual knowledge

When we speak of joy like this, we do not mean the same thing as when we speak of happiness. Happiness is a feeling and is generally considered the opposite of sadness. We feel happy when the weather suits us, when we succeed at our goals, or when we win at a game. But joy is deeper. Joy is not a feeling; joy is knowledge. We know that God is with us, and our assurance of this is based on "spiritual knowledge" that we catechists help our students come to have. It's a knowledge that comes only through faith. It cannot be acquired in any other way.

And this is our fourth lesson from Jesus: like he did in his very person, we offer our students the spiritual knowledge that God is with us. Those who have faith *know* that the light has come into the darkness and that the darkness will never overwhelm it. Light always beats the dark. We *know* that love is stronger than hate and that hope will, in the end, edge out despair. We *know* that dying always leads to new life. Yes, when we surrender and sacrifice ourselves out of true love for God and others, when we give up our life, when we take up our cross, when we walk with Jesus in this profound way, it leads to deep and amazing joy. This is the mystery of faith, the paschal mystery.

The Paschal Mystery

When we speak of the paschal mystery, we refer to the belief that God brings new life out of suffering and death. By his life, death, and resurrection, Jesus showed us the pathway to this new life: it is to die to our selfishness and embrace self-giving love.

And dying to self like this leads to a joy that remains with us even when life is difficult. We know how the faith story ends; we have peeked at the back of the book. There will be fulfillment, and we know this. We will rise again. We will live forever. Even when we fail to follow Jesus closely enough and wander into selfishness and sin, Jesus stands by, ready to pick us up and restore us. Knowing that Jesus loves us so much and stands ready to forgive us so endlessly is what keeps us coming back to him. His mercy has no end. His love is unconditional. Knowing this is the key to faith, but this is not something you can learn by simply reading about it. Such knowledge comes only through an encounter with the person of Jesus Christ.

TEACHING ABOUT THIS LOVE

As we said above, such knowledge takes time to absorb, as Jesus himself seemed to know. Like him, the people whom we teach may not yet glimpse it fully. It may require us to witness again and again. It may be the second or third year of formation before they glimpse the great hope and amazing power of divine love. For many people, deep faith comes with more maturity. We tend to grow into this knowledge rather than be zapped by it.

And there is quite a significant risk in believing that such love is offered to us. As we said above, we must give up our alternative security measures, such as money, power, or hanging on to possessions. This is risky. What if we're wrong? What if there is no God? What if all these promises from God are empty and hollow? It takes faith to do this. We catechists, like Jesus, are the models of such faith and trust in God. Our learners depend on us to be dyed-in-the-wool believers; they must see in us what they desire for themselves before they will follow us. And on our part, as Pope Francis teaches us in *The Joy of the Gospel*, 164, we must keep repeating this core message so that belief can become firm and solid over time.

The GDC summarizes this for us in articles 142 and 143:

> *There cannot be teachers of the faith*
> > *other than those who are convinced and faithful*
> > *followers of Christ and the Church.*
> *For its part, the ministry of catechesis*
> > *is always, therefore, inspired by faith itself*
> > *and by Christ's own teaching style.*
> *Under the guidance of the Spirit*
> > *it leads people to a true experience of faith*
> > *and gives them the knowledge that God is with us.*

This fourth lesson from Jesus has an important nuance. The knowledge of faith flows from the encounter with a person, not with a theology system, moral code, or even biblical study. We know what we do because in our prayer we hear the voice of Jesus (often through the ministry of the church). We hear him assuring us with love, forgiving our sins, reaching out, calling us, and walking with us in our daily lives. This gives us the inner assurance of faith, and this assurance is what we likewise pass on to our students.

Indeed, Saint Paul assured the community in Ephesus with words that echo this for us today:

> I pray that, according to the riches of his glory, [God] may grant that you may be strengthened in your inner being with power through his Spirit, and that Christ may dwell in your hearts through faith, as you are being rooted and grounded in love. I pray that you may have the power to comprehend, with all the saints, what is the breadth and length and height and depth, and to know the love of Christ that surpasses [human] knowledge, so that you may be filled with all the fullness of God. (Ephesians 3:16–19)

Jesus offers healing and love to all

Jairus, of course, did not know that Jesus loved him. He took an enormous risk of faith on the day he went to meet him. Enormous. He had no assurance. He knew only that the style and public presence of Jesus attracted him. He was bold in his faith because there was a lot at risk. "Come with me," he said to Jesus. "My child is sick." And Jesus answered, "I will come."

But our story is interrupted because, on the way to Jairus' house, another lesson from Jesus would be taught. This whole scene of Jairus coming to Jesus and Jesus going with him drew a huge crowd of curious people. Everyone wanted to see how this story would end, so they surged along with Jesus and Jairus, pushing, jostling, and murmuring. In the middle of all this was an unseen woman who had been ill since her childhood. She'd been robbed by her doctors, rejected by her family, and left on the streets. Like Jairus, she had come to meet Jesus that day. But unlike him, no one seemed to notice.

She thought to herself, "All I need to do is touch the hem of his cloak. That's it. I need only one brief moment." So she wrangled her way into the center of the crowd and did just that. With great, unseen faith, she reached out to touch Jesus.

HELPING OTHERS REACH OUT TO JESUS

This is the very moment of great catechesis. In our relationships with those who come to learn from us, those who have heard about Jesus and now want to meet him in person, how we help them reach out to touch him is so important. Like this woman, many people in our parishes and schools, our programs and neighborhoods, believe deep down that touching him is what they need. People want the joy of knowing Jesus and following his pathway through life: generosity, love, forgiveness, a heart for the poor, and mercy for all. They know they could have this, but something stands in their way. What is it? An old sin? A dark memory? Hurt? Pain? An unrealized desire? Illness? A dying child?

Our fifth lesson is that we believe Jesus will love and heal us no matter what. And the key in that sentence is the final phrase: *no matter what.* Nothing can separate us from the love of God in Jesus, as Romans 8:35 points out. But believing that can be very difficult. It's much easier to say, "Oh, Jesus is God." People say that all the time. But to also say "and he loves me just as I am" is the real test of faith—for us and for our students. This lesson is one we catechists must learn first, before we can lead our students to understand it.

Taking each person seriously

[Leading others to Christ] aims at a process of growth which entails taking seriously each person and God's plan for his or her life. All of us need to grow in Christ. Evangelization should stimulate a desire for this growth, so that each of us can say wholeheartedly: "It is no lon-

ger I who live, but Christ who lives in me" (Gal 2:20).
[*The Joy of the Gospel*, 160b]

It takes a lot of nerve to realize what sinners we are and yet to also believe that we can turn to Jesus with our whole heart, trust him, and let him welcome us into his arms. We ourselves are like the man with the sick child or the woman with the illness. We too want to touch Jesus and be healed.

But like this woman, the people in our programs sometimes must come forward without much fanfare. They're sitting in our pews, attending our classes, and volunteering in our soup kitchens. But they are carrying burdens, often for many years, and they don't know how to give these burdens to Jesus. They're anonymous, like this woman, except for one thing: *Jesus knew she was there.* "Who touched me?" he asked. His disciples thought he was mad. "You're surrounded by crowds jostling, talking, pushing, and shoving, and you're asking who touched you?" they asked him incredulously. "For heaven's sake, dozens of people have touched you!"

But Jesus knew faith when he saw it; in this woman he saw the seed of faith planted in the good earth. She came forward, telling her whole story, and he loved her for it. "You took the risk of faith," he told her. "Blessed and happy you will be."

Meanwhile, Jairus must have stood there, beside himself with anxiety. He came to get Jesus, and now Jesus was busy healing someone else. And in fact, while this whole commotion was going on in the streets, people came from Jairus' house to tell him that it was too late; his daughter was dead. Jesus overheard this and said to Jairus, "Just trust me on this." And once they arrived at the house and Jesus was able to be with the girl, he called her forth from her bed, and she was fully restored to Jairus.

This is the point at which catechesis works. Both of these

people, the woman with the illness and the man with the sick child, were called to Jesus. God had this plan for their lives, calling them both to wholeness and healing. This call didn't come out of the skies. No doves descended to direct them. No booming voices came out of the clouds. But, having heard the initial message and watched the crowds around Jesus, they heard their call embedded in the details of their own daily lives. They took the risk of faith and went to meet Jesus. Once they met him, their lives were changed forever. As Paul said, it was no longer this woman or that man who lived, but Christ who lived in them.

HELPING OUR STUDENTS

For us catechists, we learn to imitate Jesus here. As our students come forth, not sure what they will tell us but wanting the deep joy of knowing what we know, we help them encounter Jesus Christ by encountering us and our unconditional love, forgiveness, and assurance. We are the hands and feet of Christ today. Lesson five teaches us to embrace and welcome our students with the confidence that comes from knowing we do this in the name of Christ.

As the GDC puts it in articles 145-146:

> *Genuine catechesis helps discern the action of God*
> *in the life of the believer*
> *through a climate of listening, thanksgiving, and prayer.*
> *It likewise encourages active participation*
> *among those to be catechized.*
> *God speaks to us in ways we can understand.*
> *Likewise, catechesis must seek a language*
> *that effectively communicates the word of God.*
> *Only by God's grace can this be done.*
> *The Holy Spirit gives us the joy of doing it.*

We accompany our students on a journey of faith

As you think back to the previous lesson, think also about how each of your learners, no matter what their age, lives with a similar personal history and the same fears about meeting Jesus that Jairus or that woman with the illness had. We come to Jesus from the midst of our lives, not from outside of them. Whatever is happening in our lives is what faith is built on.

What is happening in the lives of the people in your class or learning group? Have they been ill? Is their home filled with fighting and tension? Are they unpopular among their peers? Do they feel they're all alone on their spiritual journey? Has their son or daughter stopped speaking to them for some reason? Have they felt condemned by the church? Rejected by society? Misunderstood by their contemporaries?

Or are they supported fully by their friends and family? Are they happy in their daily lives? Are they succeeding in their plans? Are they on good terms with their contemporaries? Are they accepted for who they are and living with a sense of well-being?

Whatever is happening in the lives of your students is important. You can't simply open up their heads and pour doctrine into them. Their lives are the good soil that is needed for the seed to sprout into full-fledged faith. Once planted, faith must be cultivated. This task of cultivating faith is our work as catechists. Lesson six is that our task is to walk with each learner and help each one go and meet Jesus, to encounter him today.

In *The Joy of the Gospel,* Pope Francis calls this by the term "accompaniment." We accompany our learners on their journeys; we become their companions for the journey of faith. "In a culture paradoxically suffering from anonymity and at the same time obsessed with the details of other people's lives...," he wrote in article 169, "the Church must look more closely and sympathetically at others whenever necessary."

Catechists and teachers can help their learners to experience the amazing presence of Christ, the pope said. Jesus is close to us, but only a companion can point him out. "The Church," Pope Francis went on to say, "will have to initiate everyone—priests, religious, and laity—into this 'art of accompaniment' which teaches us to remove our sandals before the sacred ground of the other (cf. Ex 3:5). The pace of this accompaniment must be steady and reassuring, reflecting our closeness and our compassionate gaze which also heals, liberates, and encourages growth in the Christian life."

Accompaniment

In music, the one who accompanies another player works in the background, allowing the player to shine and providing a supporting musical role. Likewise in catechesis, we accompany our learners without dominating or overwhelming them; they are the ones who must shine!

Once again, we turn to Jesus to learn how to accompany others, this time in the Gospel of Luke. Much time had passed since Jesus the master catechist had started teaching his followers about his message. At times they seemed to understand and celebrate what Jesus was telling them, but at other times they seemed as dense as logs about it all. We're out in the middle of Luke now, chapter 11, halfway between the cradle and the cross, the birth and the death of the Lord. Jesus had just spent some lovely time with two old friends, Mary and Martha. Their little household spat had ended with Jesus encouraging Martha not to fuss quite so much and to pay more attention to what really matters, as Mary was doing.

After this, and maybe inspired by what they heard about Mary and Martha, his disciples had asked him to teach them how to pray as he did. With his customary patience, he shared his way of praying and then assured them that, if they do pray, God will not disappoint them. Be persistent, he seemed to be saying, and the door will open to you. You don't have to make bargains with God, he taught. There aren't any tricks involved, no "hide-and-seek" games. Simply be direct.

Such teaching on prayer seemed to come from the soul of a man who was himself in touch with his divine Father in very intimate and personal ways. He spoke from his heart, not spinning theories on prayer but actually sharing his own way of speaking and listening with God. No doubt, Jesus was frank with his Father. They shared a love that was like no other.

The lessons on the power of God and the call to discipleship just kept coming from him, one after the other. Each lesson was rooted in the powerful truth that God loves us, even while we are still living in darkness. Jesus forgives us and takes us into his embrace as sisters and brothers, sons and daughters of God. The Spirit comes to us, he taught, a Spirit of light and love, to enlighten us with the inner assurance of faith.

His stories were penetrating and memorable. His kindness and love were palpable. He traveled with them, guiding, cajoling, and even scolding sometimes. But it was always done with generous and amazing love. He was direct and powerful in his teaching, confronting the conventional wisdom and calling everyone, including religious leaders, to practice what they preach.

HOW TO BE COMPANIONS

When we accompany others on the journey of faith, therefore, we do so in the midst of their daily lives. The church has long encouraged everyone to pause daily for an examination of conscience, looking back over one's shoulder and peering into the events, people, and situations of daily life in order to find there the presence and action of God or our own sinfulness— or both. We take our human experience very seriously, and it must also find a home in our catechetical sessions.

This lesson teaches us that we become companions to our students in more ways than one. The GDC speaks of two methods for teaching and recommends them both. The first is called "inductive" or "experience-based," and by it we begin teaching with such things as biblical events, liturgical acts, events in the church's life, or events in daily life so as to discern the meaning they might have in divine revelation. What is God telling us through these events and people? What word is being spoken to us? This method has many advantages because it matches the way God has chosen to reveal the divine mystery to us down through the ages and in the very life of Jesus Christ. It also connects to a profound human urge to know the mysterious through visible signs. When we accompany our students through catechesis, we examine their experiences and enlighten them with the word of God (GDC, 150).

The second method of teaching mentioned in the GDC is just as valid and must be in balance with the first. It is called "deductive" or "doctrine-based." The deductive method explains and describes doctrine and principles first. One then comes to understand experience by understanding how doctrine or church traditions elaborate human life. We seek the truth that is found within our beliefs, and this truth is then applied to life. This approach is also sometimes called "descending" precisely because it begins with Scripture, doctrine, or liturgy and applies them to life (GDC, 151).

As we accompany others in catechesis, these two methods should be in balance. We must teach clearly about the doctrines and customs of the church while at the same time trusting and respecting the human experiences of our students and connecting faith with life.

JESUS SHOWS US THE WAY

In one of Jesus' most famous catechetical moments, he used both of these methods, and we should learn from him to do so as well. We're in chapter 5 of the Gospel of Matthew; Jesus has gone out to a hillside or small mountain, and the crowds have followed him. His fame had spread throughout the whole area because his message was filled with hope, and the people found him to be authentic because he lived what he taught. The image of Jesus teaching from this mountain was reminiscent of Moses: Moses taught God's commandments from a mountain in the desert, and he too was a great catechist.

The gist of Jesus' message in the sermon he gave on that mount was that the kingdom of God to which he pointed was unexpectedly upside-down. Rather than having kings and rulers, armies and power, or riches and wealth, the kingdom of Jesus would be built on service, compassion, mercy, and even weakness. But his method of teaching was to connect the "doctrine" of this new kingdom with the "experience" of human life. What a wise catechist he was!

The Beatitudes, for example, are short lessons on how to respond with faith when the circumstances of life seem dire and difficult. They teach doctrine without sacrificing the experience of the learner. Mere doctrine, unconnected to spirituality and daily life, is lifeless and tasteless. For example, when Jesus taught about being poor in spirit in Matthew 5:3, he reminded his learners that being in hopeless situations in life can actually lead us to trust more in God. One translation of this verse puts it like this: "You're blessed when you're at the end of your rope. With less of you there is more of God and his rule" (*The Message*).

As we accompany our students and learners on their journeys, we certainly should teach them that believing and trusting in God is our doctrine, as this Beatitude teaches. But we should also teach them to see how this plays out when they face difficult situations in daily life. In those difficult circumstances, we become "poor in spirit" and "rich in faith."

In another of the Beatitudes, Jesus teaches us to trust in him and grow in the knowledge that he is with us even when we mourn the death of someone near and dear to us. *The Message* translates verse 4 like this: "You're blessed when you feel you've lost what is most dear to you. Only then can you be embraced by the One most dear to you." Again in this Beatitude, our doctrine of God connects with human experience.

Lesson six, then, reminds us that we aren't merely passing on a body of doctrine; we're also walking on a daily journey of faith with our students. When we accompany others on the journey to the heart of the Lord, we help implant faith into daily life. The GDC speaks clearly about this in articles 152-153:

Human experience is where faith becomes most real.
First, it arouses interest, questions, hopes, and fears...
Catechesis has the task of making people more aware
of their most basic human experiences
so they become aware of God's hand in their lives.
Second, human experience points to the divine
because there is an inborn hunger for God
in every human heart.
Reflecting on experience is therefore necessary
if the truths of Revelation are to be understood at all.
Third, experience is, in fact, the very place in human life
where salvation occurs.
The catechist must teach the person
to read his or her own lived experience
so as to see how God saves us.
In this regard, the great questions of life
are most able to lead one to the divine heart:
the existence of God,
the destiny of the human person,
the origin and end of history,
the truth about good and evil,
the meaning of suffering, love, and the future.
Interpreting and illuminating human experience
through the eyes of faith, even when difficult,
is how the revealed message and human experiences
connect and lead one to faith.
This has been true in the proclamation of the prophets,
the preaching of Christ himself,
the teaching of the apostles,
and the whole history of the Christian Church.

LEARNING FROM JESUS' TEACHING STYLE

The GDC describes Jesus' teaching style, as we saw in lesson one. In Jesus' words, signs, and works during his brief but intense life (the GDC tells us in articles 139-140), the disciples had a direct experience of the fundamental traits of the "pedagogy of Jesus." When we speak of "pedagogy," we mean the way in which Jesus approached those who came to learn from him. What was his style and method? How did he communicate and announce the message that was his to teach? We call this bundle of teaching methods by the name "pedagogy."

> ### Pedagogy
> The art of teaching is known as pedagogy. As we develop our teaching style, we learn to create life-preparing lessons—such as social skills, virtues, and values—and pass them on to those whom we teach.

As catechists, we each have a pedagogy. It may not be conscious to us but, like everyone does, each of us has developed a certain style and approach to our ministry. Our style and pedagogy play a vital role in how we accompany students on their journeys of faith. Just as a great singer needs a strong and accomplished piano accompanist, so do our students. What we provide is not musical accompaniment but spiritual companionship.

Pope Francis addressed this with great force in *The Joy of the Gospel*. "Although it sounds obvious," he wrote in article 170, "spiritual accompaniment must lead others ever closer to God, in whom we attain true freedom."

Elsewhere in the document the pope refers to those who accompany in this fashion as "companions"; this sounds very much like the sort of catechist Jesus was with his disciples.

In Spanish, the word "companion" is even more beautiful; it is rendered as *compañero*. The meaning in Spanish jumps off the page with intimacy and warmth. To be a *compañero* means, literally, "to break bread with another." Our student companions are the ones with whom we break bread, both literally and figuratively. We share meals, we share in the Eucharist, we break open the word of God, and we lead them to the ministry of the church.

Prayerful pause:
Pray for your students

1. Pause for a moment and think about each of the learners in your program. What is their story? How can you accompany each of them most effectively? Think about ways in which you can "take seriously each person and God's plan for his or her life" (*The Joy of the Gospel*, 160).

2. Begin by writing down each of your students' names, and bring to mind each face in your circle of learners. If you are a new catechist who has not yet met your group, simply anticipate in your imagination who will be with you. If you are a parent, think about your spouse and children. If you are a pastor or parish worker, consider those whom you serve. If you're a parishioner seeking to reach out, bring to mind those in your circle to whom you are called to announce the gospel.

3. Now take your time with these names, faces, or anticipated learners. Dwell with them as a mother hen would brood over her chicks.

4. When you are ready, turn your heart to Jesus and become aware of his presence. Listen to him as he calls you. "Bring your friends and learners to me," he is saying. "My arms are open and ready to accept and love them all. There is no fear here, only tender love." The Holy Spirit works within you and within your learners in order to create a desire for growth. You are the catalyst of that process.

5. Let your prayer continue until you seem to reach a conclusion. Then close by letting your heart swell with gratitude.

Jesus teaches us to be servant-catechists

The purpose of this companionship with others, as Pope Francis tells us, is to stimulate within them a desire to grow in their faith, to grow in their practice of self-giving love, and to grow in the ways in which they imitate Christ. If we consider how Jesus himself did this, we find some outstanding clues to help us find our own way. Lesson seven is that, as teachers, we are not the "commanders" or "bosses" of our students, but we are their servants.

An excellent example of Jesus the servant accompanying his disciples on their journeys of faith comes to us in chapter 13 of the Gospel of John. Here we meet Jesus having supper with his friends. We must remember that this is not their first supper; they had been eating together for many years. They were, indeed, companions. They knew each other well, and they were familiar with a shared supper routine, much like the one anyone would have in daily life.

When Pope Francis asks us catechists to become companions to our learners and students, he is asking us to play a role like the one Jesus did in his community. Here in chapter 13 of John, we witness Jesus as servant-catechist demonstrating (not just talking about) his love for us.

Chapter 13 of John unfolds during a difficult period in their lives as disciples, friends, and followers of Jesus. All the signs around them pointed to imminent disaster, and Jesus himself had been talking about his own death. His followers must have been reeling from what had happened just days before: Jesus had ridden triumphantly into Jerusalem on a donkey, but his disciples had not fully understood what was happening. They may even have expected him to lead some kind of army into town, but here he was on a donkey. How utterly confusing! Afterward, Jesus spoke once again about his impending death and, again, the disciples seemed mystified by it all. Jesus had tried to explain it: "Unless a grain of wheat falls into the earth and dies, it remains just a single grain," he had told them in John 12:24. "But if it dies, it bears much fruit."

"What could this mean?" they must have thought.

Jesus' own soul was troubled now, as we are told in John 12:27. He was ready to accept death even if the crowds and his own closest friends did not fully understand, but he knew it would not be easy. All the events of his life were culminating in these final moments, and he was quite alone. Not even a voice from heaven (12:28) helped his followers comprehend how death could lead to life. I'm sure it was frustrating for Jesus that his followers did not seem to understand him.

Now in chapter 13, they're all having supper, and Jesus knows that the Father has put all things into his hands. Jesus seems to have decided that the time for words and doctrinal lessons was over and that it was time to demonstrate more dramatically what it means to be the servant and to die to oneself. This is the "last supper" as John tells it. The focus is not on the institution of the Eucharist (as it was in Matthew, Mark, and Luke) but on something else. Jesus is the master catechist once again. He really loved his friends, the text tells us (verse 1), and he wanted to teach them one last time what it means to embrace his message.

Like we catechists experience with our students sometimes, Jesus struggled as a catechist to find the right language with which to help his disciples understand that we are called to die to ourselves and that only such death will lead to new life. Like our students, his disciples needed time to let all this sink in, and the events in Jerusalem were unfolding quickly now. The end was near.

Now, mind you, Jesus had spent many years trying to get this message across. He had patiently walked with them as their companion. He had used parables, images, and instruction. He had shown them by his own life. So with little time remaining, Jesus chose this tender moment at supper to demonstrate once more his great love for them—and for us.

He got up from the table, according to the text of John, took off his robe, tied a towel around his waist as an apron, poured water into a bowl, and began to wash their feet. He washed their feet! In the first century, when Jesus lived, feet were dirty. There were no shoes, only sandals. The streets were full of garbage, mud, and manure. Washing someone else's feet was seen as very demeaning. Household slaves were expected to do it for their owners. And yet here was Jesus doing it for his disciples. This is what it means to die, he was teaching them. This is how you serve one another, how you become companions for each other.

What a lesson! Jesus was truly the master catechist.

FOLLOWING JESUS' EXAMPLE

Jesus' action that night provides a job description for us as catechists. After he finished going around the circle, one by one, including the initially reluctant Peter, Jesus drove his point home explicitly. He said to his disciples, "Do you know what I have done to you? You call me Teacher and Lord—and you are right, for that is what I am. So if I, your Lord and Teacher, have washed your feet, you also ought to wash one another's feet. For I have set you an example, that you also should do as I have done to you" (John 13:12b–15).

The seventh lesson from Jesus, then, is that we are called to become servant-catechists. Indeed, when Pope Francis asks us to accompany others, to become their companions on the journey of faith, he is asking us at the same time to embrace the example of Jesus and "wash their feet" as a way of serving them. Pope Francis points out that such service is what will lead them to faith—and haven't we seen Pope Francis himself do this time and again? This is what it means to die to ourselves. Of course, today we have shoes and more hygiene. It isn't necessary to literally wash feet. But the call to be servant-catechists remains strong nonetheless. Jesus' example is the one we follow today.

So how does lesson seven play out in our daily or weekly ministry settings? What does a servant-catechist do that others don't? The answer lies in that story about Jesus and the disciples' feet. We metaphorically remove our fine clothing, put on an apron, and tend to each of our students. We begin by knowing each one's name, their family setting, and the context in which they live. We gently prod and lead them to awareness of their own selfishness (the obstacle to faith) and also to how much Jesus loves them and how often he forgives them. We give up our time, our money, and our privacy to be with them in class, to provide them with kindness, and to share with them from our own lives. We consider them a great and wonderful gift, and we are aware of the honor it is to serve as their catechists—rather than seeing our ministry as a duty, a drudgery, or a demand. We bring them by name into prayer often, opening ourselves to how God might lead us to approach and respond to them. In a word, we dedicate ourselves to them as a servant would do to the ones for whom he or she works.

Our goal is to help our students meet Jesus

In *The Joy of the Gospel*, Pope Francis points out that we do not measure spiritual growth and intimacy with Christ mainly in terms of knowing the doctrine of the church (161). Knowing doctrine does not always help people encounter the Lord and walk with him in their daily lives. It doesn't always lead people to wash each other's feet or to carry their cross.

When we speak of doctrine here, we include all of those dogmas, customs, and teachings of our faith that are contained in the *Catechism*. They are certainly important, but they are not the only aim of catechesis or faith formation, and this is a big change in focus for us.

Responding with love

It would not be right to see this call to growth [in faith] exclusively or primarily in terms of doctrinal formation. It has to do with "observing" all that the Lord has shown us as the way of responding to his love. Along with the virtues, this means above all the new commandment, the first and the greatest of the commandments, and the one that best identifies us as Christ's disciples: "This is my commandment, that you love one another as I have loved you" (John 15:12). [*The Joy of the Gospel*, 161a]

Here is what the GDC tells us about this in article 98:

Jesus Christ not only transmits God's word,
Jesus is that word;
and all catechesis is completely tied to him.
What does this mean?
It means that what we find at the heart of all catechesis
is not a book or a theology system,
but a person!
The fundamental task of catechesis is to present Christ
and everything in relation to him,
leading people to follow Christ in their lives.

As Pope Francis calls us catechists and teachers to become companions to those whom we teach, we must bear this reality in mind. We are not passing on a mere body of information and doctrine; we are helping our learners come to know Christ and to live as he taught us to. Following the example of Jesus, the way we treat our students and the way we guide them is vitally important. Our students, for their part, must be invited into the learning process.

The GDC describes our students for us. Here's what it tells us in article 157:

Those to be catechized cannot be passive recipients
but must be actively engaged in the process
through prayer,
participation in the sacraments,

> *the liturgy,*
> *parish life,*
> *social commitments,*
> *works of charity,*
> *and the promotion of human values.*
> *Catechesis, after all, is a process of taking on a way of life*
> *and personal conversion,*
> *not the acquisition of a body of information.*

Lesson eight teaches us that our chief task is to lead our students to see Jesus' loving heart. This is how they will "see Jesus." To do that, we engage in a sort of dialogue with our students. The dialogue will include words exchanged in conversation, of course, but it also includes the non-verbal exchange between what we see in our students and what they see in us. They need to meet us and see into our faith. This means we must sometimes put down the textbook in order to show our learners what's in our own hearts; this is the mandate. Sharing our own faith as a catechist is the chief way in which we become companions to our learners.

SEEING CHRIST IN ONE ANOTHER

Our textbooks are loaded with doctrinal details. Every page is crowded with facts, quotes, and very correct doctrinal formulas. It's all there on the page, in black and white and color. In graphics, boxes, paragraphs, and definitions, everything we teach is presented. And yet meeting Jesus can't be put down on a page. Becoming aware of what keeps us away from him, admitting that sinfulness and taking the first step toward him, as did Jairus and the woman with the illness, just can't be taught from the pages of a textbook. There is an element of personal witness involved in this, of telling our own stories, of letting people see how God has touched our own lives.

In understanding the eighth lesson here, we realize that our own lives as Christians and catechists shine for all to see. No matter what's in the textbook, our students meet Christ through us. We must, likewise, see Christ in them.

In article 156, the GDC puts a fine point on this:

> *Nothing—not the method, or the texts,*
>   *or any other part of the program—*
>   *is more important than the person of the catechist*
>   *in every phase of the catechetical process.*
> *The gifts given to the catechist by the Spirit*
>   *to witness faithfully and live accordingly*
>   *are the very soul of catechetical ministry...*
> *Because of this, the catechist is called to a Christian way of life*
>   *that reflects his or her beliefs well.*

Pope Francis teaches that the call to faith flows from observing all that the Lord has shown us as the way of responding to his love. We catechists must help our students see love—and learn to practice self-giving love. Our own lives are the example of this. How has God loved us through thick and thin, in good times and in tough times, as a sinner or a saint? Our learners must observe this in us before they can learn to follow that pathway themselves. This is how they meet Jesus.

At one point in the Gospel of Mark, this lesson is driven home to us in a powerful and personal way. We are in Jericho again, seventeen miles outside of Jerusalem, and Jesus will ride triumphantly into town on a donkey only a few days later. The text of this story is at the end of chapter 10 in Mark. Jesus and his entourage are leaving town, presumably to go to Jerusalem, but Jesus has a lesson of love to show to the people before he goes. A blind fellow named Bartimaeus is sitting alongside the road. He was a beggar, we are told. Like so many others in that region, he had heard about Jesus. The key to the story is the fact that he wanted to meet Jesus.

This is that moment when catechesis is possible. We tell our students about Jesus, about his love, his mercy, his forgiving heart—and we get them excited to know him. Knowing him changes our lives forever. And as Pope Francis has reminded us, once they do surrender to the care of Jesus and the ministry of the church, our students will find out that Jesus does not disappoint them.

So Bartimaeus, blind as a bat but believing like a member of the choir, starts calling out for Jesus. He had no other choice. "Son of David," he hollered, "have mercy on me." Those in charge of this crowd told him sternly to shut up, but he would have none of that. He just called out more loudly. Jesus, seeing this, seemed to find it remarkable, because he stopped, called the fellow over to him, and offered him the mercy he was asking for. In the text of this story, we are told that once Jesus spoke to him, Bartimaeus threw off his coat, threw off whatever was weighing him down. The text uses important words to say what happened next: "he sprang to his feet," we are told, and came to Jesus. One can only spring to one's feet when excitement, freedom, and hope make that possible. Bartimaeus sensed that he was close to having freedom from his blindness; hope arose in his heart; and he was certainly very excited indeed. Who wouldn't be?

"What do you want?" Jesus asked. And what Bartimaeus asked for is what our students ask of us. "My teacher," he said, "I want to see." And Jesus' response to him is the response our students wait for. "Your faith has saved you," Jesus told him.

LISTENING AND RESPONDING TO OUR STUDENTS

Our ears as catechists must be open to hear when our students call out to us from the roadside of life. What freedom are they asking for? How can we offer it to them? What mantle hangs around their neck holding them down? Is it an old sin? Is it a violent culture? Is it the harsh judgments of others because of their personality, temperament, or other trait? Is it fear of being made a fool? Fear of losing everything?

And when they do call out to us, then we respond as Jesus did. We reveal our own inner journeys and the ways in which faith has worked in our lives, giving them hope. When we do this, we should use language and examples that are appropriate to our group in terms of age, stage of life, and context. We might reveal more in the context of a retreat than in a classroom, or we might share certain things with a small group of adults that we would not share with eight-year-olds, but in every case we should see ourselves as companions to our learners, walking with them as Jesus did and sharing with them at a deep level.

From Pope Francis

[Such catechesis] has to express God's saving love which precedes any moral and religious obligation on our part; it should not impose the truth but appeal to freedom; it should be marked by joy, encouragement, liveliness, and a harmonious balance which will not reduce preaching to a few doctrines which are at times more philosophical than evangelical. All this demands on the part of the [catechist] certain attitudes which foster openness to the message: approachability, readiness for dialogue, patience, a warmth and welcome which is non-judgmental. [*The Joy of the Gospel*, 165b]

We are called to speak clearly about forgiveness, to call people to generosity, to take enormous risks in loving and embracing the poor, and to love our enemies without bombing them or seeking revenge. Our witness to these truths should be so clear that it draws people in. Others should see in us the truths they also seek.

In sum, lesson eight teaches us that the Christian journey is more a journey of growth in love than it is growth in understanding theology. Theology and doctrine can elaborate love, but love is always first, as Pope Francis said. Saint Paul taught this in Galatians where he wrote about his desires for the people in that community. He prayed that meeting Jesus would cause them to increase and abound in love for each other and everyone around them. Everything we know about God's word is summed up in this, and true freedom and happiness flow from it.

Grace flows only from God's generous heart

In lesson nine, Jesus the master catechist reveals to us that God implants within us the gift of grace, and only by that grace can we respond in faith. Jesus was constantly responding to the faith that he found within the people who came to him. "Your faith has saved you," he often told people.

In fact, the ninth lesson teaches us that the entire process of hearing the call, responding in faith, and growing in love is always preceded by God's free and generous gift of grace. In Ephesians, Paul explains it like this: "For by grace you have been saved through faith, and this is not your own doing; it is the gift of God..." (2:8).

Saint Paul based this teaching on the many stories from the life of Jesus in which he pointed out this grace and faith. One of the most dramatic stories is found in chapter 7 of Luke. Jesus had gone to eat supper at the home of a leading religious figure. He was seated at table with the other guests, and dinner was about to get underway, but a woman, an uninvited guest, came to see Jesus. She came to see Jesus because she was aware of her own sinfulness and his power to forgive her. To demonstrate her faith, she washed his feet; once again, the washing of feet is a key symbol. She kissed them and anointed them with a fine lotion. When the Pharisee objected, Jesus excoriated him because the woman had offered him greater hospitality than he had. Then, turning to her, Jesus said, "Your faith has saved you; go in peace."

Jesus made no pretense of having implanted the faith within her. Faith like this is a gift that comes to us through the work of the Holy Spirit. Jesus observed it and, by his affirmation and assurance, strengthened that faith. This woman was experiencing grace.

The grace that this woman experienced, the power to be aware of her sinfulness and to seek forgiveness, is gift. It's free, and this is difficult for us to believe sometimes. We want to believe that we have to earn God's love, or that somehow we must be good first so grace will come to us. In fact, it is grace that enables us to see divine love in the midst of our selfishness and to adopt that love as our own lifestyle.

The lesson for us is that our students are also being given the gift of faith; they also are being offered grace. We don't implant such faith but, like Jesus, we strengthen and affirm it.

A WORD ABOUT GRACE

There were many reforms at the Second Vatican Council, but perhaps the most fundamental of them all is that the Council helped restore how we speak about grace. On the eve of the Council in the 1960s, living in the state of grace was the goal of the Catholic life. And it goes without saying that dying in the state of grace was the only way to heaven. This grace, we believed, was "dispensed" by the church; we may have believed that only Catholics could get it. There was a popular sense that one could "earn" it. And in our thinking about it we sometimes muddled it up with indulgences as though the two were the same.

But because of work done at the Council by bishops and theologians such as Yves Congar, Karl Rahner, and Cardinal Leo Joseph Suenens, among others, we have restored to the church a much more ancient understanding of grace, rooted in Scripture and full of God's generous love. Our restored understanding of grace, our new horizon on it, has significantly changed how we go about the business of catechesis and faith formation.

From Pope Francis

On the other hand this process of response and growth is always preceded by God's gift...The Father's free gift which makes us his sons and daughters [is] the gift of his grace (cf. Ephesians 2:8-9; 1 Corinthians 4:7)...In this way, we allow ourselves to be transformed in Christ through a life lived "according to the Spirit" (Rom 8:5).
[*The Joy of the Gospel*, 162]

Grace is God communicating God's own loving self to us (*Catechism*, 1966-1974). It is offered to everyone, to every human, not just to Catholics. Indeed, to be conceived is to be offered grace. It's experienced as a loving, divine energy (or power) that fills our bodies and our souls. It's absolutely free, and it cannot be earned. It comes from God alone. The church doesn't so much "dispense" it as lead us to discover it by providing "moments of grace" through liturgy, social action, and, of course, through catechesis and faith formation.

And what is the effect of grace? Put simply, it "lets us be" who we're made to be, which is precisely how we eventually reach heaven, by being who God intends us to be.

HELPING STUDENTS DISCOVER THE PRESENCE OF GOD

Now here's the key for us catechists in lesson nine: grace is active and powerfully present in the lives of those ten-year-olds we face every week in the religious education program. God, in other words, is acting in the lives of those kids. God is not absent or distant. God is there and active. God loves those children, even when they misbehave. And the same goes for youth and adults at every age and stage of life. So no matter what else we do with our students, helping them discover the presence of God is always our first goal.

Our task, therefore, is not merely to teach *about* God or the church, and certainly not to *bring* God to them, or try to *make God present*. It is, rather, to help people realize that God is already present in their lives, loving and forgiving them, waiting for them to turn to him. God is seeking to reveal himself to everyone, and that revelation comes through the ones (like us catechists) called to echo such faith in our lives. The grace our students experience empowers them to become the persons in life that they are created to be.

Prayerful pause:
Listen as you prepare your lesson

Providing catechesis that cooperates with God's grace in the lives of our students is a tall order. It was much easier when we were only expected to teach what was on the page of the textbook, wasn't it? We could deliver the details, test the children on it, and go home. Job done. But now we're expected to bring our own heart and story into the teaching. We're expected to become companions to our learners, to walk with them on the journey of faith. Here are five steps to help us get started and succeed at doing that.

1. Pause for just two minutes and turn your heart to Christ. Pause at your desk, in your car, or wherever you are and become conscious of the presence of Christ near you. He is there. You do not need many words for this. You can be present with Christ and recognize Christ's presence with you in the same way that you are near your spouse or dear friend in a quiet moment: not speaking, simply being near one another, sensing the presence of the other, glowing in your love, contemplating your bond. This two-minute pause begins it all.

2. Be aware of your own failures to love, your selfishness, your self-taking actions and sinful attitudes. Be aware of how you have ignored the suffering and poor, how you have judged others harshly, or treated others without love. Your own "unworthiness" is a lynchpin in understanding the powerful and overwhelming love that Christ

has for you. His love is not dependent on your goodness but on the divine source of love.

3. Let this wonderful, unconditional divine love wash over you. In your heart, let the arms of Christ surround you; hear him speak words of mercy and forgiveness. You may want to celebrate the Eucharist or the sacrament of reconciliation as a way of celebrating how God's love fills you.

4. Listen now for the call. You are called to lead others to Jesus, to help them find this same moment. How is that call sounded in your life? In what ways are you also called to imitate Christ and practice self-giving love? In what people, events, or situations is this call embedded? Think about the people you are about to catechize, and offer yourself to Jesus as an earthen vessel, a means by which he will reach them with this saving message. Shed your own self and put on Christ like a garment. Open yourself to grace flowing through you, empowering others to love.

5. Prepare your material. Whether you use a textbook, DVD, PowerPoint, handouts, or other resources, review and prepare what you will teach. In all of it, let these moments with Jesus remain front and center. Open yourself to the ways in which you can insert an appropriate image or story, or ways in which you can invite your learners to share their stories. Once your preparation is complete, return to Jesus in prayer and end with the awareness that he remains with you even when you are not conscious of his presence.

10

Jesus teaches us to announce his love and forgiveness

Jesus, according to Mark chapter 6, understood people's hunger. The crowds were "astonished" at what he taught them, even though he was, like you or me, just a common person. Jesus also understood his own need to rest and be alone but it was often difficult to find that solitude. Here in chapter 6, after seeking a "deserted place...to rest a while," a large crowd of hungry people were fed by both his word and the sharing of bread and fish. His disciples had been clueless about how to feed such a large crowd. They had suggested that the people be sent off to fend for themselves. They could not imagine that they could be the ones called to such a ministry until Jesus instructed them with these words, "You give them something to eat."

After this meal, they returned to the work. More crowds. More hungry people. More preaching. One day they sailed across the lake to Bethsaida where Jesus restored sight to a blind man, a slow becoming-able-to-see. As with his disci-

ples—and as with our own students and learners—faith often
needs time to ripen and mature.

According to chapter 7 in the Gospel of Mark, Jesus and his
disciples went north on one occasion into the vicinity of Tyre
and Sidon, seaport cities on the Mediterranean quite far away
from Galilee. It seems they wanted a few days of rest and a little distance from the crowds. Their work had become intense
in recent weeks: Jesus had just dealt with the violent death of
his cousin John the Baptist, fed thousands in the desert who
had come to hear him teach, assured his own closest friends
that the storms of life could be calmed, and excoriated the
religious leaders for their thin faith. This must have been an
exhausting period of Jesus' ministry. Wherever they went, the
people came asking for healing; there was no escape.

So north toward Tyre and Sidon they went, into the home
of someone where they thought they could hide. But word
about him and his amazing powers had reached even this re-
mote place, and a Greek woman came to the house, requesting
healing for her daughter. Jesus refused her, saying his message
and healing were meant for the Jews. But she would not give
up, and Jesus, impressed by her faith, eventually relented.

Then once again they found themselves traveling on the
road, this time to Caesarea Philippi, a Roman town north of
the Sea of Galilee. We're in chapter 8 of the Gospel of Mark
here, the very center of this gospel. As they walked and talked
together, Jesus turned to his disciples to ask one of the most
personal and pithy questions in the gospels. It seemed to come
from the heart of a man who was sorting out his own destiny and identity. What are people saying about me? he asked
them. "Who do people say that I am?"

This is the sort of question one might ask of his or her closest friends during a public time of life and ministry. A parish

priest might ask it as he preaches prophetically, calling people to die to themselves as they imitate Christ. A catechist might ask it as she accompanies her students on their pathway of faith, calling them to grow in love and revealing her own inner life in the process. A person working for justice and peace might ask it as he demands integrity and honesty from government or church leaders. The pope himself may ask it as he leads the church into a deeper sense of mercy and a growing sense of love.

On that lonely road and dusty day with Jesus, the master catechist, Peter answered on behalf of us all. "You are the Messiah," he said. We believe that you are the Christ, sent by God.

THE CRUCIAL QUESTION: WHO IS JESUS?

The lesson for us catechists here is that we too must ask the right question. For us catechists and teachers, this same question looms before us: *Who do we say that Jesus is?*

The answer we give to this question is central in all our preparation. Our answer should be considered carefully, for at the heart of all catechesis is the announcement we make about Jesus Christ. In *The Joy of the Gospel*, Pope Francis makes this a central point. The first and main thing we should teach, he says, is about Jesus. We don't teach first about the church, or about the pope, or about the Scriptures, or even about morality. These latter things are all meant to elaborate the deeper reality that stands behind our faith—the very person of Jesus Christ. Our tenth lesson comes from Jesus through Pope Francis:

> On the lips of the catechist the first proclamation
> must ring out over and over: "Jesus Christ loves
> you; he gave his life to save you; and now he is liv-

ing at your side every day to enlighten, strengthen, and free you." This first proclamation is called "first" not because it exists at the beginning and can then be forgotten or replaced by other more important things. It is first in a qualitative sense because it is the principal proclamation, the one which we must hear again and again in different ways, the one which we must announce one way or another throughout the process of catechesis, at every level and moment. [*The Joy of the Gospel,* 164b]

We call this "first thing to teach" by a Greek term in the church: *kerygma.* This is an ancient term that means, literally, "to proclaim something great!" It refers to the Holy Spirit, who is given to us; the Spirit in turn helps us come to know Jesus Christ, who, by his self-giving love, teaches us about the infinite mercy of the Father. Kerygma is a term that is largely unfamiliar to most average Catholics but it is a term we catechists and teachers must learn. Put simply, the kerygma is the very heart of the gospel, the core message of the Christian faith that all believers are called to proclaim by their lives as well as their words.

THE HEART OF WHAT WE DO

Every catechist in every aspect of parish ministry is called on to proclaim this kerygma message: "Jesus Christ loves you unconditionally. His self-giving love on the cross counters and outweighs all your own self-taking, your own sinfulness. He is present to you now in your daily life, implanting the Holy Spirit within you, leading you to see God's great mercy." Good news, indeed!

This core message or kerygma must be laced into everything else we teach, and this is our tenth lesson. For as Pope Francis insists, we should not think that we can proclaim this once and for all and have it over and done. The core message here isn't something we teach in order to get it out of the way so we can proceed to more "solid" formation. "Nothing is more solid," he said in *The Joy of the Gospel*, 165. "Nothing is more solid, profound, secure, meaningful and wisdom-filled than that initial proclamation."

This kerygma message of the presence and love of Jesus in our lives illuminates everything else we teach. If we are teaching about the sacrament of baptism, the kerygma must be present in what we say. Baptism by itself is nothing without the light that Jesus brings to us through it. If we are teaching about attending Sunday liturgy, caring for the poor, understanding the love of neighbor, or studying the Bible, this core kerygma message must be in that. "It has to express God's saving love which precedes any moral and religious obligation on our part" (*The Joy of the Gospel*, 165).

Kerygma

All Christian formation consists of entering more deeply into the kerygma, which is reflected in and constantly illumines the work of catechesis, thereby enabling us to understand more fully the significance of every subject that the latter treats. [*The Joy of the Gospel*, 165]

Such a proclamation should not impose the truth on others or emerge from a "better than thou" attitude, according to the pope, but it should appeal to freedom. Only in knowing Jesus can we be truly free. Only when we shed ourselves and imitate the self-giving love of Jesus can we be free to really love recklessly. We have nothing to lose if we have given it all up freely in the first place.

CATECHISTS: LIVE THE GOOD NEWS!

The one proclaiming this (that's you and I as catechists or active Christians) should be seen by all as full of happiness and good humor. This is good news, after all, not a grim message of duty and burden. The learning environment should reflect this. It should provide gentle and generous hospitality to people, an open door, a reduction in rules and procedures that are difficult to follow, and a sense of lightness. We are announcing to others that, if they turn their own heart to Christ, he will not disappoint them. He will reach back with mercy and endless forgiveness. It is amazing and unforgettable to realize that he forgives us and calls us even though he knows full well our own lack of love.

When we learn to turn to him in this way, we hear Jesus comfort and assure us: "I have always loved you and have never left your side. You are my beloved one; I offer you my love even when you reject it and try to go your own way. But now I invite you once again to live with self-giving love for others and yes, even for yourself. Invite those whom you know to come to me with their burdens and pain. I am here for them all."

11

Faith is our response to the announcement of God's love

One of the most important elements of the kerygma or core message that we should not overlook is our response to it. We respond to the generous and amazing divine love by imitating it. We die to ourselves as Jesus did. So, embedded in the kerygma is a vocation given to each of us, a call to "take up our own cross" and follow Jesus on the way. This dying to self is our call to holiness. Jesus' mother, Mary, received this call and responded in turn: I understand, she said to the angel. I get it. I will give myself up and do what God asks.

This is the faith response. Our students can only respond with the assent of faith if they first hear the announcement of the kerygma from us. This puts a strong obligation on our part to be effective in making such an announcement, and that is what this eleventh lesson teaches us. It teaches that the purpose of continually reminding our students that Jesus loves them, that he died for them, that he forgives them, and that he now walks with them, is to tease out a response of faith.

So the kerygma isn't just a bit of theology we master in order to gain technical understanding; it's much more than that because it leads to a life-changing faith response on the part of the Christian: "Yes, Lord. I will be the big one. I will put the last first. I will include the poor. I will stand before you humbly acknowledging my sinfulness. I will be part of your family. You will be my God and I will be your son or daughter. I will choose life over death, love over hate, and kindness over harsh and judgmental attitudes toward others. Yes, Lord, in light of your love I will also love. I open myself to your Spirit and enter into your community of love. I will show the mercy of the Father. Yes, Lord."

THE EUCHARIST AND THE KERYGMA

How we teach about the Eucharist, for example, should lead others to faith. We don't teach about it only in order to explain it academically. We should ask, therefore, how the kerygma is laced into what we teach about the Eucharist. Is the essential truth of Eucharist not that Christ loves us? That Christ's self-giving love on the cross continues to save us from our own selfish tendencies? That Christ is truly here, present with us in profound and meaningful and life-changing ways? Mere doctrinal formulations that do not include this core message are dry and lifeless, even though they are true. When you teach about the Eucharist, make sure your lesson points to the kerygma.

In the Gospel of Luke, chapter 22, we meet Jesus at that famous last supper, and we hear and see him reaching out to his disciples with love and compassion. This was a profoundly personal moment in their lives, a tender and final meal. We should be careful not to treat it as a mere theological idea.

NURTURING A CLOSE CONNECTION TO JESUS

When teaching about the Eucharist (or anything else), you should reach a point where you put the book down and invite your circle of learners to talk together with you as their companion about how the Eucharist demonstrates the love that Jesus has for us. Through the Eucharist, Jesus walks with us in our daily lives. Invite your circle of learners to revisit the Eucharist and kindle in themselves a closer connection to Jesus. In this sacramental moment, he connects us to each other as the body of Christ and offers us his own very self as nourishment. Share your own experience of this.

This is the moment at which you can introduce your students to eucharistic prayer. We do not merely "attend the Mass," but we take an active and conscious role in celebrating it. We don't go to Mass so much to get something out of it as to donate ourselves to each other as a community. We go to Mass for each other, not for ourselves.

Here is where you can help your students learn to bring to Mass the prayer that their hearts may be open to hear the word and to share the Eucharist in ways that change their lives. The same is true for you. What is in your own heart that you need to place on the altar with the bread and wine? What sorrow, worry, joy, or satisfaction do you bring to God? Here is where you can help make the Eucharist personal for your students, not merely a large public event. You can help them make it personal without making it private. It is a shared personal moment in which God touches us with the power of grace.

THE TRINITY AND THE KERYGMA

Or, for another example, how is the kerygma laced into what we teach about the doctrine of the Trinity? Do we not believe that the Trinity leads us to understand the unconditional love of God? Doesn't the Trinity point to the fact that, when we live in love, we live in God? Doesn't this belief lead us to the understanding that God is not far away; that God does not reside in some sort of Trinitarian heaven-beyond-earth, but that God is amazingly close, loving us here and now, even as you read this very line? Is not the core message about the Trinity that we ourselves have been invited by God to live in that divine community of love?

TEACHING ABOUT THE MYSTERY OF GOD

Therefore, when teaching about the Trinity, you can help your students understand that the Trinity is not floating out in the stars somewhere, up above our heads, absent and distant from us. It is as near to us as a turn of the head, a glance of the eye. When we live in love, we live *within the Trinity*. Perhaps no doctrine leads to a clearer understanding that Jesus loves us and is present with us. Nothing teaches more clearly than this that the mercy of the Father is offered to us. The Spirit opens our hearts to see all this in the message of the kerygma.

This is your chance to help your students understand the mystery of God in a new light. The Trinity is not some abstract theological proposition. It is a description of the community of God, the family to which we belong. When we profess faith in the Trinity, we profess faith in love; they are one and the same. Here is a chance for us to help our students make this connection and understand the kerygma: "Jesus Christ loves you, he gave his life to save you, and now he is living at your side every day to enlighten, strengthen, and free you."

THE HEART OF WHAT WE DO

All the elements of our doctrinal belief, our biblical studies, and our moral and social teachings spring from this core proclamation, this kerygma. And all catechesis must lead back to that as well. Article 98 of the GDC, which we saw above, puts it like this, in summary form: Jesus Christ not only transmits God's word; Jesus is that word, and all catechesis is completely tied to him. What does this mean? It means that what we find at the heart of all catechesis is not a book or a theology system but a person! The fundamental task of catechesis, the GDC goes on, is to present Christ and everything in relation to him, leading people to follow Christ in their lives.

This eleventh lesson teaches us that, in bringing the kerygma into all catechesis, we draw out of the student an attitude of interest and openness to the experience of knowing Jesus closely. It's faith! As catechists, therefore, we must be patient and consistent, open to dialogue with the learner, and non-judgmental as we welcome everyone warmly into the faith. These attitudes of patience and kindness toward the learner flow from the message itself. When our learners can see evidence that such faith is present in our lives as catechists, then the core message is alive and exciting! This is our challenge as catechists.

Listening to our students opens the door of faith

Remember that story about Bartimaeus that we explored earlier? Or remember the one about Zacchaeus in his sycamore tree? Remember when Jairus came to Jesus asking for help with his sick daughter? Or how about the woman who came to wash his feet at that big, fancy dinner party? Or the Greek woman who requested healing for her child in Tyre?

What did we learn from Jesus, our master catechist, in all these teaching moments? How did he treat the people who came to him? We can put it into one word. He *listened*. Jesus listened carefully to the people who came to him. He really heard what they said with their words, but also with their hearts and lives.

Here is our final and important lesson from Jesus. It's one that reaches deep into our ministry as catechists and teachers. When Pope Francis calls us to be companions to our students, he is urging us to imitate Jesus "the master listener." It's very tempting when we're holding a textbook to become the sort of teacher who is over-and-above the learners, the "one in the know," the expert, and the only one in the room who speaks. But what kind of companion would we be if we were the only ones who spoke? How would it be for everyone else to merely "sit and listen" except when called on to answer a question? Companions don't do all the talking; the talking is a conversation. So a large element in our pedagogy is to listen carefully to our learners.

When we listen to our students, we open the doorway of faith for them, just as Jesus did for those who came to meet him in person. Only in letting our students speak in order to process and absorb what we teach can we lead them to Jesus. Jesus himself had this openness of heart; once again, he is our master catechist.

In one stunning example of this, we find Jesus already on the cross, but still teaching us how to live, forgive, and die. Hanging there in such pain, one could have forgiven him for attending to his own agony. But instead, he listened to those who remained with him, whether by force or out of love. That thief who approached him, for example, could have merely annoyed Jesus. But Jesus listened to him intently, according to Luke 23:42–43. He read his heart and offered him mercy. Isn't that just stunning? Such listening is the hallmark of successful catechesis. Without it, we just plough on, dumping material into our students' heads without regard for their own ability to receive it.

Listening

"We need to practice the art of listening which is more than simply hearing. Listening, in communication, is an openness of heart which makes possible that closeness

without which genuine spiritual encounter cannot oc-
cur." [*The Joy of the Gospel*, 171]

Openness of heart. This is a skill that is essential in catechesis. The open heart provides a safe place for the learner to experience the presence of Jesus. It's that sense of being close to our students that creates the environment in which faith is free to grow. Like dinner mates, a catechist-companion listens closely to hear how the word is received by each learner.

"Listening helps us to find the right gesture and word which shows that we are more than simply bystanders," Pope Francis went on. "Only through such respectful and compassionate listening can we enter on the paths of true growth and awaken a yearning for the Christian ideal: the desire to respond fully to God's love and to bring to fruition what he has sown in our lives."

LISTENING IN CATECHESIS

Face your students, look at them, and maintain eye contact.
If your student is talking to you and you're busy trying to read ahead in your text or even looking out the window, not much communication will happen. At home, if the person were your child, you might demand, "Look at me when I'm talking to you," but that's not the sort of thing we say in the context of religious education. Do your students the courtesy of turning to face them. Put aside papers, books, your mobile phone, and other distractions. Look at them, even if they don't look at you.

Be attentive, but relaxed.
Now that you have given your student your full attention, you can relax without staring at them and making them uncomfortable. You can look away now and then and carry on like a

normal person. The important thing is to be attentive. Have in the back of your mind that your student is on a spiritual journey and you hold the map. They're asking you for directions. So don't be distracted by anything else.

Don't judge.
Listen without judging your student or mentally criticizing the things you're hearing. If you hear something a bit alarming, go ahead and feel alarmed, but don't judge them as bad, stupid, or unholy. Don't jump to conclusions as you listen. Give them the chance to explore faith on their own. Remember, faith grows little by little in the heart of the believer.

Don't interrupt, and don't jump to "easy solutions."
The person speaking to you may be having an awakening or a crisis of faith, but let them finish what they have to say. Don't offer simple solutions or platitudes. Simply let them feel that you heard them and that you love them. Most people really aren't asking for advice. They simply want to be heard. Most students just need you to listen. And above all, don't be a sentence-grabber, interrupting and finishing their sentences.

Ask questions only to ensure understanding.
Be careful not to jump in with your own experiences and ideas. Don't speak in order to demonstrate how much you know about the question. Just let your student share their thoughts and questions, and only speak to affirm that they have been heard.

Try to feel what the speaker is feeling.
You will do well as a listener if you show that you hear them being sad when the person with whom you are talking express-

es sadness, that you hear them being happy when they express joy, and so forth. Sharing about faith often leads to emotional experiences, and your empathy is the heart and soul of good listening.

Keep loving them.

Even if the person sharing with you tells you something that is upsetting, be sure your own heart remains loving toward them. Nothing is gained by turning away from love. Your unconditional love reflects God's forgiveness and love. As a catechist, echoing God's love in this way makes you truly successful.

Listen at their speed.

There is always a temptation in catechesis to simply "dump the details" on our learners, to read through the lesson from front to back without regard to any questions they might have, any resistance they might be feeling, or any moving moments of insight that our learners might experience. The idea that our task in catechesis is to "get to the end of the lesson" is challenged by the pope's call to become companions to our learners first and foremost. We are walking in faith with them, and that requires that we move at their speed, not at ours.

Listen with patience.

Such companionship requires great patience on our part, and great trust in the Spirit that what is needed for each learner will unfold in the right time for them. Our pedagogy as catechists should be characterized by this patience. We unfold the mysteries about which we teach little by little. There is need, Pope Francis wrote in article 171, for a pedagogy that introduces learners step by step until they grasp the mystery of God more fully. "Reaching a level of maturity where individuals can make truly free and responsible decisions," he wrote, "calls for much time and patience. As Blessed Peter Faber used to say: 'Time is God's messenger.'"

Listen through a conversational style.
As a catechist, then, you can learn to move slowly enough that your students can keep up with you. Most lessons that we teach have far too much material in them even for adults, much less for children. One excellent skill that helps you do this is to develop in your pedagogy a "conversational style." Such a style allows your group of learners to integrate and personalize what you teach. It allows them to do some of the talking! In a conversational pedagogy, you would always begin your lesson by inviting them to respond to a personal question. Then you build any "content" on their stories and experiences, connecting and linking it to them as you go. Throughout the lesson, you pause here and there to allow your learners to observe things, ask questions, and do more talking.

Listen by looking back.
And before you end your session, you pause once again to revisit what you have just done. You look back over your shoulder at what you just did in this lesson, go back over the key points briefly, and then ask your learners what they heard and what insights they take home from it.

This final pause at the end of your lesson is a very helpful element in a "listening pedagogy." Simply pause and look back at what you just taught or what your group just experienced in prayer, liturgy, or content. You briefly revisit or review your lesson, which many good teachers already do. But then you ask your learners to speak up and say what word, idea, insight, or image in this lesson caught their ear. What touched their heart? What led them to feel close to Jesus? Give them time to speak, and really listen to them when they do.

A "listening" style of teaching reflects the patience and steady example of Jesus, the master catechist.

Prayerful pause:
Begin and end in prayer

Get Ready

As you get ready to teach, it is important that you immerse yourself in the presence of Jesus. We have to find time to do this in the midst of many other family, job, or school commitments. I know you're busy. The end of the day comes before you know it! But find a short time, maybe ten minutes, to just sit. Here are some strategies to help you make this happen:

- If you have children at home and they're being loud after a day of school, can someone else tend to them for a while?
- If not, then leave a bit early for your religious education, RCIA, adult ed, or school teaching work. Arrive early enough to sit in the chapel.
- If you don't have children but life is moving fast, you can slow it down. Turn off your TV. Hit the pause button on the iPod. Just turn off the darn computer.
- If silence troubles you, pay attention to that. Let the thoughts that come to you enter your mind as welcome thoughts. But set each aside, turning your heart again and again to prayer.

Start Thinking

- You're going to be encountering a group of learners—no matter what their age. A very important reality is part of this: God is acting in their lives! God is acting! Wow! Here are some points to help you get started in this prayer:

- The everyday experiences of the ones whom you are about to teach are very important. Their experiences are loaded up with the possibility that it could lead them to see God. You can help them in this process.
- Think about your own day. How did God touch you today? Think back over the day from the first things you did until now. If it's morning, think back over last evening, event-by-event and person-by-person.
  » Whom did you meet, even for a moment?
  » Who called on the phone?
  » What did you see on TV—news or programming?
  » Who were you with, or with whom did you wish to be?
- Each of these is a possible way in which God is touching you now.

Now Let's Pray
Let your thoughts return again and again to Christ, to the Holy Spirit, to God who is both Mother and Father to you right now.

Begin by tracing on your body the sign of the cross.
    Jesus Christ, my friend and brother,
        you are the one I want to reveal
            to my students today.
    I believe in you—help me to believe more!
        From your Holy Spirit I have received
            the gift of teaching.

Thank you for this great gift.

Pause to recall your various experiences of teaching in the past.
But am I worthy?
You know my sinfulness!
You know my weaknesses!
How could you have possibly chosen me?
I'm getting ready now to teach
but I need your help!
Without your love and power within me
I can do nothing whatsoever.
Let everything that happens in this teaching time
lead them and me to you. Amen.

PRAYING AFTER CLASS

Finishing the Job
When you have completed the work of teaching, there is a final step you must take in order to "finish the job." You must return to the Lord now with your whole heart to thank God for his wonderful works. Even if you feel the teaching went badly, you cannot see who may have been touched or how God's hand may have reached out to someone in this period.

Pour yourself a cup of coffee or cold drink and spend time now with God.

Being Thankful
For what are you thankful in this time?
- Which learner seemed to blossom today?
- What words formed themselves on your lips as a complete gift from God, allowing you to speak of faith with clarity?
- What new insight did you have about faith?

- Which of your teaching plans unfolded with grace and ease?

What did you resist in this time?
- Which of your students do you resist?
- What aggravations did you experience while you were teaching?
- What points of faith were more difficult for you to teach?

Now let's pray.
Find a quiet spot for yourself. It may be late at night or early in the morning, but be sure it is within a few hours of your teaching time. Perhaps it is in the car on the way home as you recall your teaching experience and consider it in your mind. Pray in these or similar words:

Jesus, teacher of all and source of faith;
 Spirit of God, living within me,
  sustaining and supporting me,
   giving me the gift of teaching;
I open my heart and mind to your presence.

Here pause to allow the memories of the teaching period just ended to come to mind. Review carefully the flow of the teaching, the content, the people, each face, each moment, and each response from a learner. Allow your thoughts to roam around in these memories for a short while.

Thank you for working through me
 to touch these learners.
I praise and honor you for the amazing work
 you have done through me.

I myself am honored to be called for this work
and I gladly offer it to you now.
If in this teaching,
there were ways in which I resisted your word
I surrender them now to you.
Forgive me for failing to trust completely in you,
and help my faith to grow.
I know you are with me
and you behold all I say and do.
Grant, by the light of your Spirit,
that I may be earnest
in my search for truth,
and fair in how I treat others. Amen.

Study Guide
for Group Use

FOR EACH LESSON:

1. Read each lesson before your small group convenes. Begin here with the Sign of the Cross. Plan to have a cup of coffee or glass of wine on hand to make this time fun and friendly.

2. Each of you should restate the lesson learned in your own words. You may want to write down a concise statement to summarize the lesson, making sure you fully grasp the meaning. Share this statement with others in your group.

3. Tell one way in which you find this lesson challenging, using an example from your experience as a catechist, teacher, parent, or friend to others.

4. Now tell about how you hope to incorporate this lesson into your own style of teaching and leading others to faith. Be specific. What will you change in order to make

this lesson come alive for you? What is Jesus saying to you through this lesson?

5. Now share as a group the Scripture story on which this lesson is based (see the guide below). Read that story aloud in your group. Pause at the end and share with each other what image, word, feeling, or memory this story evokes for you.

6. With that story in mind, take a couple moments of quiet in your group. Each of you should write down or rehearse a line or two of prayer. After the brief quiet pause, close by sharing each person's brief prayer, moving around the circle until everyone has shared.

SCRIPTURE STORIES

Lesson 1: Luke 19:1–10 *Zacchaeus*

Lesson 2: Mark 4:1–9 *The Sower*

Lesson 3: Mark 5:21–43 *Jairus and the woman who sought healing*

Lesson 4: Ephesians 3:16–19 *Spiritual knowledge*

Lesson 5: Romans 8:31–39 *Nothing can separate us from the love of God*

Lesson 6: Matthew 5:3–11 *The Beatitudes*

Lesson 7: John 13:1–15 *The washing of the feet*

Lesson 8: Mark 10:46–52 *Bartimaeus*

Lesson 9: Luke 7:36–50 *The contrite woman*

Lesson 10: Mark 8:27–30 *Who do people say I am?*

Lesson 11: Luke 22:14–23 *The Last Supper*

Lesson 12: Luke 23:39–43 *The thief who asked for mercy*